VETERAN2FED

The No-BS Guide to Landing a Federal Job After Military Service

A Straight-Talking Guide for Veterans Ready to Serve Again

BY

LARRY J. LOCKE Sr.

Veteran2Fed
MISSION: YOUR NEXT FEDERAL CAREER

For permission requests, contact the author at:

info@veteran2fed.com

First Edition

ISBN: [979-8-9998250-0-1]

ISBN (ebook): [979-8-9998250-0-8]

Published by Locke, Larry Veteran2fed Publishing 2191 Canyon Stream Drive, Sierra Vista, Arizona 85635

Website: Veteran2Fed.com

Printed in the United States of America

Library of Congress Control Number: 10987654321

This book is dedicated to every veteran who has served with honor and is ready to serve again in their next mission.

Table of Contents

Preface

Why I Wrote This Book

When I retired after 23 years in the Army, I thought I had it all figured out. I had the experience, the leadership, the logistics expertise — I had the résumé in my head, the drive in my chest, and the belief that my next chapter would fall into place.

Then the rejection emails started rolling in. Over and over again, I saw the same words:

"Not among the best qualified."

That line hit harder than I ever expected. Not because I doubted myself — but because for the first time since I was 18, I felt invisible. After decades of serving my country, I couldn't even get past the first round of a hiring system that was supposed to welcome veterans with open arms.

I knew I wasn't the only one. I knew there were thousands of veterans just like me, sitting in front of a computer late at night, wondering why the system didn't see their value. That's when I decided to do something about it.

This book is the guide I wish I'd had when I was in that spot — frustrated, confused, and wondering if I'd ever land a federal career. It's not a silver bullet. It's not filled with empty promises. It's the real, no-BS truth about what it takes to make the transition successfully.

If you come here looking for sugar-coating, you won't find it. What you will find is a roadmap, built from hard-earned lessons, mistakes, and wins — all designed to help you get where you deserve to be.

Because here's the truth:

You already did the hard part. You served with honor, you led with grit, and you carried the mission when it mattered most. Now it's time to make sure that service translates into a career that honors your sacrifice and secure your future.

That's why I wrote this book. Not to tell my story, but to help you write yours.

— Larry Locke

About the Book

After years of service, too many veterans run into the same frustrating wall: rejection emails that read "Not among the best qualified."

In Veteran2Fed, U.S. Army veteran Larry Locke delivers a no-nonsense roadmap to navigating the federal hiring system. Drawing on 23 years of military service and his own hard-won lessons from transitioning into federal work, Larry breaks down the barriers that keep veterans from landing the jobs they've earned.

This guide shows veterans how to translate their military experience, crack the USAJobs system, interview with confidence, and thrive in federal service — all while keeping their sense of mission and purpose alive.

Key Takeaways

- Why veterans struggle in the federal hiring process — and how to overcome it
- The truth about federal résumés (and why "short and sweet" doesn't cut it)
- How to interview like you already belong there
- What to expect after the job offer — and how to thrive in federal service
- How to redefine your mission beyond the uniform

Introduction
From One Veteran to Another

If you're holding this book, chances are you've already had that moment — the day you took off the uniform and wondered, now what?

I know the feeling. After 23 years in the Army, I thought I had everything lined up. I knew my MOS cold. I'd led soldiers, managed millions in equipment, and mastered logistics from top to bottom. But when I started applying for federal jobs, the rejection emails started piling up:

"Not among the best qualified."

It didn't matter that I'd spent decades serving my country. On paper, I wasn't even making the cut.

That's when I realized the problem wasn't my skills. The problem was translation. The federal hiring system didn't understand the language of my service. And unless I figured out how to speak its language, I was going to stay stuck.

That's why I built Veteran2Fed — and why I wrote this book.

This isn't a sugar-coated pep talk or a 200-page résumé template. It's a no-BS roadmap from someone who's been there. Inside, you'll learn why the system feels broken, how to stop wasting time with trial and error, and what it really takes to go from "Not among the best qualified" to "Congratulations, you've been selected."

Because here's the truth:

You didn't serve your country just to struggle on the sidelines now.

You've already proven yourself. You've already led, sacrificed, and delivered when it mattered most. Now it's time to take that same grit and turn it into a federal career you've earned — one that supports you, your family, and your future.

Let's get started.

— Larry Locke

Founder, Veteran2Fed

Chapter 1
The Great Divide — Military Out, Now What?

There's a moment every veteran knows too well: the day you hang up the uniform for the last time. You smooth out the wrinkles, check the ribbons one final time, and close the closet door. The silence that follows isn't just quiet — it's the sound of everything you've known for the last 20+ years coming to an end.

For months, maybe years, you've been counting down to that moment. You tell yourself, I'm ready. I've got skills. I've led people, managed missions, and handled more stress before breakfast than most folks do in a week.

Then reality smacks you in the face.

You're out. No more formation. No more chain of command telling you where to be and when to be there. No more marching orders dropped in your inbox at 0500. It's quiet now — a little too quiet. And for the first time in a long time, it's 100% on you to figure out the next move.

That silence? That's the sound of the transition.

The Hard Truth About Transition

Most veterans think the hard part is behind them — and who could blame them? After all, if you can handle three-hour sleep cycles in a combat zone, navigate military bureaucracy, and keep your cool when everything's falling apart, how hard could civilian job hunting be?

The answer: tougher than you'd think.

Because the truth is, transitioning out of the military comes with its own battlefield. It's not the kind with sand, sweat, and 100-pound rucksacks. It's the one with résumés, online applications, job boards that feel like mazes, and rejection emails that read like copy-and-paste breakups.

And here's the kicker — you're competing against civilians who've been playing the federal hiring game for years. They know the system. They know the jargon. Meanwhile, you're staring at a job posting with "GS-0346-12" in the title wondering if that's a job code or the password to launch a missile.

Why Veterans Get Passed Over

Here's what the numbers don't tell you: 67% of veterans say the federal hiring process is their biggest post-service frustration. Not finding housing. Not adjusting to civilian life. Getting ignored by the very government they served.

Here's the part nobody tells you: the civilian world doesn't always know what to do with you. They see "Squad Leader" or "Platoon Sergeant" on your résumé, and they have no clue that means you managed 40 people, $10 million worth of equipment, and operations that would make a corporate manager cry into their coffee.

To them, it's just a line they don't understand. And because they don't understand, your application gets filtered into the black hole of USAJobs — you know, that place where résumés go to die.

So what happens?

Veterans — good ones, qualified ones, mission-ready ones — get passed over. Not because they can't do the job, but because they don't know how to translate what they've done into something HR can understand. And let's be real — nobody in uniform ever pulled you aside and said, "Here's how you write a killer federal résumé."

The Divide Is Real

Here's the part nobody wants to say out loud:

The system isn't set up to roll out a red carpet for you. You've got to kick the door in yourself.

That's the divide. On one side: the military — structured, predictable (mostly), with a clear chain of command and mission. On the other:

civilian federal service — full of opportunity, but with its own confusing rules and language.

Crossing that divide is where a lot of veterans stumble. Some get discouraged. Some settle for jobs far below their potential. Some give up on the federal path altogether, thinking, maybe it's just not for me.

But let me tell you something: it is for you. You've already proven you can thrive in demanding environments, solve problems under pressure, and lead people from all walks of life. You've been tested in ways most of your future coworkers can't even imagine. You belong in federal service — not as an afterthought, but as an asset.

You Already Have What It Takes

Here's the good news: you don't need to start from scratch. You already have the skills, the grit, and the discipline to succeed. What you need now is a roadmap — a way to navigate the federal system without getting lost in the shuffle.

Think of it like a new mission. The objective: land the federal job that matches your experience and sets you up for the career you deserve. The obstacles: a system that doesn't make sense, résumés that need a translator, and interviews that feel like they were designed to trip you up. The good news? Missions are what you do best.

That's what this book — and Veteran2Fed — is about.

I built Veteran2Fed because I got tired of watching sharp, capable veterans get left behind. I know the frustration. I've felt the sting of thinking, Why am I not getting picked up? I also know the satisfaction of finally breaking through and stepping into a federal career where your skills, your leadership, and your service mean something.

What's Ahead

In the chapters ahead, we'll cut through the noise and give you the no-fluff truth about:

- How the federal hiring process actually works (and why it feels like a maze).
- How to package your military experience so it gets noticed.
- The insider tips for acing interviews without feeling like you're selling your soul.
- And most importantly — how to not just land the job, but thrive once you're in it.

So take a breath. The uniform may be hanging in the closet, but your mission isn't over. It's just evolving. And this time, the mission is you.

Because here's the bottom line:

You didn't survive deployment stress, master complex logistics, and lead people under fire just to get filtered out by some HR software that doesn't know what a platoon sergeant actually does. You earned the right to serve again — this time in a career that actually supports your life instead of consuming it.

Chapter 2

Understanding the Federal Job Jungle

What You're Up Against — and Why It's Not Your Fault

Welcome to the jungle — and no, not the one from the song. This jungle has worse predators: automated screening software that doesn't understand what a platoon sergeant does, HR specialists who think 'logistics' means delivering pizza, and a hiring system so complex it makes military bureaucracy look streamlined.

If you've ever spent an afternoon on USAJobs.gov, you know what I mean. It feels like trying to read a foreign language through a foggy windshield — while it's raining. On fire.

It's not set up to help you. It's set up to screen you.

But here's the truth: once you understand how this beast works, you can navigate it like a pro. And more importantly, you can stop wasting time and energy wondering what's wrong with you. Because nothing is wrong with you — the system is just built different.

The Language Barrier No One Warned You About

Let's get this out of the way: the civilian hiring world does not speak military. You might be a seasoned NCO or an officer with decades of leadership and logistics under your belt — and the system still won't "see" you unless you speak its language.

Here's what I learned the hard way:

After 23 years in the Army, I knew logistics top to bottom. I was an expert in all nine classes of supply, led soldiers, moved missions forward, and solved problems that would make a project manager cry. But when I submitted those first résumés, the message came back the same way every time:

"Not among the best qualified."

That was the wake-up call. It wasn't about what I'd done — it was about how I was saying it.

USAJobs Is a System — Not a Person

One of the biggest mistakes veterans make is thinking a human being is reading their résumé. Most of the time, they're not — at least not at first.

USAJobs runs like a filter. You upload your résumé, and software scans it looking for keywords that match what's in the job announcement. If your résumé doesn't match the language of the posting? You're out.

Doesn't matter if you ran supply ops bigger than FedEx — if you didn't say it in the right way, you're invisible.

How the Automated Screening Works:

1. Job announcement gets posted with specific keywords and requirements
2. Your application gets uploaded to the system
3. Software scans your résumé for keyword matches
4. Applications get ranked by keyword density and relevance
5. Top-ranked applications get passed to human reviewers
6. Only the "best qualified" make it to the hiring manager

The Filtering Reality:

Here's the brutal math: Typical federal job posting gets 400+ applications. Only 50-75 make it past the keyword robots. Maybe 20 get reviewed by humans. And only 3-5 get interviews. Your résumé must survive three different elimination rounds before a human being even knows you exist.

Your résumé must survive multiple cuts before a human even sees it.

Federal Hiring Timeline: Managing Your Expectations

The Real Timeline (Not What They Tell You)

Job Announcement Phase:

- Posted for 5-30 days (varies by position)
- Applications close at 11:59 PM on closing date
- Late applications automatically rejected (no exceptions)

Initial Screening Phase (2-4 weeks):

- Automated keyword screening
- Basic qualification review
- Veterans preference points applied
- "Best qualified" list created

Human Review Phase (2-6 weeks):

- HR specialist reviews qualified applications
- Subject matter experts may provide input
- Interview list finalized (usually 3-10 candidates)
- Security clearance verification begins

Interview Phase (2-8 weeks):

- Interview scheduling (coordination nightmare with panels)
- Interviews conducted
- Reference checks
- Selection decision made

Offer Phase (1-4 weeks):

- Tentative offer extended
- Salary negotiation (if applicable)
- Final offer and start date coordination

Total Time: 2-6 months from application to start date

Veterans often get frustrated and think they've been rejected when they're actually still in the process. Federal hiring moves at federal speed.

Agency Breakdown: Where Veterans Succeed

Not all federal agencies are created equal when it comes to hiring and supporting veterans. Here's the inside scoop:

Top Veteran-Friendly Agencies:

Department of Veterans Affairs (VA)

- Veteran hiring preference: Very strong
- Culture: Understands military background
- Common positions: Medical, IT, benefits processing, facility management
- Veteran percentage: ~30% of workforce

Department of Defense (DoD)

- Veteran hiring preference: Strong
- Culture: Military-friendly, understands rank structure
- Common positions: Logistics, contracting, cybersecurity, program management
- Veteran percentage: ~25% of workforce

Department of Homeland Security (DHS)

- Veteran hiring preference: Strong
- Culture: Mission-focused, security-oriented
- Common positions: Border patrol, TSA, cybersecurity, emergency management
- Veteran percentage: ~22% of workforce

General Services Administration (GSA)

- Veteran hiring preference: Moderate to strong

- Culture: Business-focused, efficiency-oriented
- Common positions: Contracting, real estate, IT, project management
- Veteran percentage: ~20% of workforce

Department of Transportation (DOT)

- Veteran hiring preference: Moderate
- Culture: Engineering and safety-focused
- Common positions: Aviation, transportation planning, safety inspection
- Veteran percentage: ~18% of workforce

Decoding Job Series: What Those Numbers Mean

Federal jobs are organized by "series" — numeric codes that group similar positions. Here's what veterans need to know:

Popular Job Series for Veterans:

GS-0080 Security Administration

- Security specialists, physical security, personnel security
- Good fit: Military police, security forces, intelligence

GS-0343 Management Analysis

- Process improvement, program analysis, organizational development
- Good fit: Staff officers, operations NCOs, any leadership background

GS-1102 Contracting

- Government contracting, procurement, vendor management
- Good fit: Contracting officers, supply personnel, logistics specialists

GS-2210 Information Technology

- All IT positions across government
- Good fit: Signal/IT personnel, cybersecurity specialists

GS-1896 Border Patrol Agent

- CBP border patrol positions
- Good fit: Infantry, military police, combat arms

GS-0025 Park Ranger

- National Park Service positions
- Good fit: Military police, outdoor leadership experience

Understanding Grade Levels:

- **GS-5 to GS-8**: Entry level, usually requires some experience or education
- **GS-9 to GS-12**: Mid-level, requires significant experience or advanced education
- **GS-13 to GS-15**: Senior level, supervisory or technical expert positions
- **SES:** Senior Executive Service, equivalent to general/flag officer level

Military Rank to GS Level Translation (Rough Guide):

- E-4 to E-6: Typically, GS-5 to GS-8
- E-7 to E-9: Typically, GS-9 to GS-12
- O-1 to O-3: Typically, GS-11 to GS-13
- O-4 to O-6: Typically, GS-13 to GS-15

Veterans' Preference: Your Secret Weapon (If You Use It Right)

Veterans' Preference gives you extra points on your application — but here's what most veterans don't understand: it only kicks in AFTER you're deemed qualified. Think of it like this: if you don't meet the basic requirements, preference points are like extra credit on a test you failed. Worthless.

Types of Veterans' Preference:

5-Point Preference (TP)

- Discharged under honorable conditions
- Served during wartime OR in a campaign/expedition
- Additional 5 points added to passing score

10-Point Preference (XP)

- 30% or more service-connected disability
- Receive disability compensation/pension/retirement from VA
- Additional 10 points added to passing score

10-Point Preference (CP)

- Spouse of disabled veteran (under certain conditions)
- Widow/widower of veteran
- Mother of veteran who died in service
- Important Veterans' Preference Facts:
- Only applies to competitive service positions
- Doesn't guarantee you'll be hired
- Must still meet basic qualifications
- Some positions are exempt (attorney, chaplain, etc.)
- Points are added AFTER you're deemed qualified

How to Claim Veterans' Preference:

- Check the appropriate box on your application
- Upload your DD-214 (Member 4 copy)
- Include VA disability letter if claiming 10-point preference
- Make sure your discharge is characterized as honorable

Special Hiring Authorities: Fast Tracks for Veterans

Veterans' Recruitment Appointment (VRA)

- For veterans with 2+ years active duty or discharged due to service-connected disability
- Allows non-competitive hiring up to GS-11 or equivalent
- 2-year trial period, then conversion to permanent
- No age limit

Veterans Employment Opportunities Act (VEOA)

- Allows eligible veterans to apply for positions typically open only to current federal employees
- Must be preference eligible OR separated after 3+ years of continuous active duty
- Expands your job opportunities significantly

30% or More Disabled Veterans

- Can be non-competitively appointed to any position they're qualified for
- No grade level limitation
- Significant advantage in hiring process
- Military Spouse Employment Partnership
- For spouses of active duty service members
- Streamlined hiring process with participating agencies
- Focus on portable careers and remote work

Security Clearance: Your Golden Ticket

If you have an active security clearance, you're sitting on gold. Here's why:

The Clearance Advantage:

Having an active Secret clearance can bump your starting salary by $10,000-15,000. Top Secret? Even more. I've seen veterans negotiate higher step levels purely because they brought clearance to the table.

- Clearance investigations cost $3,000-$15,000 and take 6-18 months
- Agencies prefer candidates who already have clearances
- Many positions require clearance on day one
- Cleared candidates often negotiate higher starting salaries

Types of Clearances:

- **Public Trust:** Lower level, background investigation
- **Secret:** Standard clearance, 10-year reinvestigation cycle
- **Top Secret:** Higher level clearance, 5-year reinvestigation cycle
- **SCI:** Compartmented information access

Maintaining Your Clearance Value:

- Keep your clearance active if possible (contracting, reserves, etc.)
- Understand when clearances transfer vs. when they need renewal
- Highlight clearance level prominently in your federal résumé
- Apply for positions that specifically require your clearance level

USAJobs Navigation: Tactical Tutorial

Creating Your USAJobs Profile:

1. Use your legal name (exactly as it appears on your ID)
2. Upload a comprehensive federal résumé (not a private sector résumé)
3. Complete all sections thoroughly
4. Upload supporting documents (DD-214, transcripts, etc.)
5. Set up saved searches for positions you want

Reading Job Announcements Like a Pro:

- **"Who May Apply"** section: Determines if you're eligible

- **Duties section:** Mine for keywords to include in your résumé
- **Qualifications section:** Must meet 100% of these requirements
- **How You Will Be Evaluated:** Shows what they're looking for in applications

Application Strategy:

- Apply within 48 hours of job posting
- Tailor your résumé to each specific job announcement
- Use the exact language from the job posting
- Submit all required documents (incomplete applications automatically rejected)

Common USAJobs Mistakes:

- Using a private sector résumé format
- Failing to address specific qualifications
- Missing application deadlines
- Not uploading required documents
- Applying for positions you're not eligible for

You've Got Advantages — If You Know How to Use Them

The good news? As a veteran, you've already earned tools that give you an edge:

- Veterans' Preference: Extra points on your application (if used correctly).
- Special Hiring Authorities: VRA and VEOA programs that can get you in faster.
- Security Clearances: If you've got one, agencies love it.
- Leadership Experience: Proven ability to manage people and resources.
- Mission Focus: Understanding of how to accomplish objectives.
- Adaptability: Proven ability to work in different environments.

But here's the thing no one says out loud:

None of that matters if your résumé never makes it through the filter.

That's where most veterans get stuck — and stay stuck. They think, "I'm a vet, so I should be good." Not true. The system doesn't reward your service unless you navigate it right.

This Isn't About Handouts — It's About Strategy

Let's be clear: you're not looking for a handout. You've already earned your stripes. What you want is a career where your skills matter, where your leadership means something, and where you can continue making an impact.

But to do that, you've got to understand the battlefield you're on now.

And this isn't a tactical mission — it's a strategic one.

You wouldn't walk into an op without intel. You'd get the lay of the land, check your gear, and have a plan. Same rules apply here.

That's what I built Veteran2Fed to do — not just tell you what the system looks like, but guide you through how to work it in your favor.

What This Chapter Won't Do (And Why That's a Good Thing)

You may notice I'm not giving you a full résumé template here, or walking you line-by-line through the application process. That's intentional.

Because here's the truth:

This book is here to open your eyes. My business is where we roll up our sleeves and get to work.

Veteran2Fed is built to walk beside you — to translate your experience, build a killer federal résumé, prep you for interviews, and keep you focused until that offer letter hits your inbox.

But for now, this chapter should've done two things:

1. Made you realize that if you've been stuck, you're not broken — the system is.
2. Made it clear that you don't have to fight that system alone.

What Veteran2Fed Does Differently

At Veteran2Fed, I don't just explain the system — I help you master it:

- **System Navigation:** Personal guidance through USAJobs and federal hiring process
- **Agency Intelligence:** Insider knowledge about which agencies are hiring and their cultures
- **Clearance Strategy:** How to maximize your security clearance value
- **Timeline Management:** Realistic expectations and milestone tracking
- **Preference Optimization:** Ensuring you get maximum benefit from veterans' preference
- **Application Strategy:** Which positions to target and when to apply

Because understanding the jungle is one thing. Having a guide who's navigated it successfully? That's how you get to your destination.

What's Next

In the next chapter, we'll look at one of the biggest barriers: how to translate your military experience into language that makes federal HR take notice.

I'll give you a peek at the common mistakes veterans make and a preview of how small changes can make a big impact. But if you want your application to actually get seen — and land interviews — that's where we go from "reader" to "client."

Because like I always say:

You already did the hard part — now it's time to get what you've earned.

Chapter 3

Translating Your Military Experience From "Sergeant Speak" to "HR Speak"

Let's be real — your military career already reads like a résumé. You've got years of leadership, specialized training, and mission success under your belt. You've managed people, resources, and situations that would make a civilian manager pass out cold.

So why does it feel like you're invisible when you apply for federal jobs?

Two words: translation problem.

The Wake-Up Call

When I retired after 23 years in the Army, I thought landing a federal job would be a slam dunk. I'd been in logistics my entire career. I knew all nine classes of supply, top to bottom. I'd been responsible for equipment worth more than some companies are on the stock market.

But when I applied for jobs, the rejections started rolling in:

"Not among the best qualified."

Over and over again.

I knew I was qualified. Hell, I'd managed logistics operations that would make Amazon's supply chain look like a lemonade stand. But every rejection email felt like a punch to the gut. What I didn't know was how to speak the system's language — and that language barrier was costing me everything.

That's when I realized the problem wasn't me. It was the translation.

Why the System Doesn't Understand You

Here's the reality: HR doesn't know what you've done. Not because you didn't do it, but because you didn't say it in their language.

- To you, "Platoon Sergeant" means you supervised 40 personnel, managed millions in equipment, and delivered results under pressure.
- To them, "Platoon Sergeant" sounds like you ran around yelling "hooah" and making people do push-ups. They don't see the budget management, crisis leadership, or complex problem-solving. They see a stereotype from a movie.

It's not that they don't respect your service. It's that they don't understand it. And unless you make it clear in their language, your résumé gets tossed in the pile.

The Translation Formula That Works

Before we dive into specific examples, here's the formula I use with every Veteran2Fed client:

Military Role + Scope + Impact = Federal Gold

- **Military Role:** What you did (but in civilian terms)
- **Scope:** How big, how many, how much (numbers matter)
- **Impact:** What happened because of your work (results, not just duties)

Here's what this looks like in practice: Instead of "Platoon Sergeant responsible for soldiers," you write "Operations Supervisor directing 40-member logistics team, coordinating training and resource allocation to achieve 98% mission success rate while maintaining $5M in equipment accountability."

See the difference? Same job, but one gets interviews and one gets ignored.

Real-World Example

Here's a simple side-by-side comparison:

Military Version:

- Served as Platoon Sergeant for a transportation unit, responsible for training, readiness, and supply distribution.
- Federal Translation:
- Directed daily operations of a 40-member transportation unit, coordinating logistics, training, and resource allocation to achieve mission objectives. Oversaw accountability and distribution of $5M in equipment and supplies, maintaining 100% readiness.

See the difference?

The first version is vague. The second spells out leadership, scope, resources, and results — all things federal HR reps are scanning for.

MOS-Specific Translation Examples

Infantry/Combat Arms Translation

The Challenge: "All I did was kick down doors and shoot things."

The Reality: You were a tactical operations specialist with leadership and crisis management experience.

Military Version:

- Infantry Squad Leader, responsible for 9-person team

Federal Translation:

- Supervised tactical operations team of 9 personnel, ensuring mission readiness and safety protocols. Coordinated with multiple units to execute complex operations requiring precise timing and resource allocation. Maintained 100% accountability of assigned personnel and equipment valued at $500K.

Key Federal Job Series for Infantry:

- Border Patrol Agent (GS-1896)
- Police Officer (GS-0083)
- Security Specialist (GS-0080)
- Emergency Management Specialist (GS-0089)

What NOT to write: "Infantry soldier with combat experience"

Why it fails: Vague, focuses on combat instead of leadership and operations management

Logistics/Supply Translation

Military Version:

- Motor Transport Operator, drove trucks and maintained vehicles

Federal Translation:

- Transportation Operations Specialist responsible for fleet management and cargo distribution across multiple locations. Maintained detailed records for vehicle maintenance schedules, reducing downtime by 15%. Coordinated delivery schedules for time-sensitive materials, ensuring 98% on-time delivery rate.

Key Federal Job Series:

- Transportation Specialist (GS-2101)
- Supply Technician (GS-2005)
- Inventory Management Specialist (GS-2010)

Medical/Healthcare Translation

Military Version:

- Combat Medic, provided medical care in field conditions

Federal Translation:

- Emergency Medical Technician with experience in high-stress environments and multi-casualty incidents. Administered life-saving medical interventions while maintaining accurate patient documentation. Trained and mentored junior medical personnel in emergency procedures and equipment operation.

Key Federal Job Series:

- Medical Technician (GS-0645)
- Emergency Medical Technician (GS-0640)
- Health Technician (GS-0645)

Intelligence Translation

Military Version:

- Intelligence Analyst, analyzed enemy threats

Federal Translation:

- Intelligence Research Specialist responsible for collecting, analyzing, and disseminating threat assessments. Prepared detailed intelligence briefings for senior leadership using multiple data sources and analytical tools. Maintained security protocols for classified information handling and storage.

Key Federal Job Series:

- Intelligence Analyst (GS-0132)
- Research Analyst (GS-1515)
- Criminal Investigator (GS-1811)

Communications/IT Translation

Military Version:

- Signal Support Systems Specialist, maintained communication equipment

Federal Translation:

- Information Technology Specialist responsible for network operations and cybersecurity protocols. Troubleshot complex technical issues reducing system downtime by 25%. Implemented security measures protecting sensitive data across multiple classified networks.

Key Federal Job Series:

- IT Specialist (GS-2210)
- Electronics Technician (GS-0856)
- Telecommunications Specialist (GS-0391)

What NOT to write: "Fixed radios and computers"

Why it fails: Doesn't show technical expertise or security knowledge

Aviation/Maintenance Translation

Military Version:

- Aircraft Mechanic, maintained helicopters and performed inspections

Federal Translation:

- Aviation Maintenance Specialist responsible for preventive and corrective maintenance on $50M aircraft fleet. Conducted detailed safety inspections ensuring 99.5% mission readiness while maintaining strict compliance with federal aviation regulations and safety protocols.

Key Federal Job Series:

- Aircraft Mechanic (WG-8852)
- Aviation Safety Inspector (GS-1825)
- Quality Assurance Specialist (GS-1910)

What NOT to write: "Fixed helicopters and did inspections"

Why it fails: Doesn't show the complexity, safety responsibility, or regulatory knowledge

Artillery/Fire Support Translation

Military Version:

- Fire Direction Control specialist, calculated firing solutions

Federal Translation:

- Data Analysis Specialist responsible for complex mathematical calculations and real-time decision support. Processed multiple data inputs to provide accurate targeting solutions under time-critical conditions, maintaining 100% accuracy in high-pressure environments.

Key Federal Job Series:

- Mathematical Statistician (GS-1529)
- Operations Research Analyst (GS-1515)
- Emergency Management Specialist (GS-0089)

What NOT to write: "Calculated artillery firing data"

Why it fails: Sounds too military-specific, doesn't translate analytical skills

Military Intelligence Translation

Military Version:

- Intelligence Analyst, analyzed enemy threats and briefed leadership

Federal Translation:

- Intelligence Research Specialist responsible for collecting, analyzing, and synthesizing complex information from multiple sources. Prepared comprehensive analytical reports and delivered briefings to senior leadership, supporting critical operational decisions affecting national security interests.

Key Federal Job Series:

- Intelligence Analyst (GS-0132)
- Criminal Investigator (GS-1811)
- Research Analyst (GS-1515)

What NOT to write: "Looked at enemy intelligence"

Why it fails: Undersells analytical complexity and strategic thinking

The Numbers Game: How to Quantify Everything

Veterans often think they can't quantify their experience. Here's how to find your numbers:

Personnel Management

- Squad size, platoon size, company size
- Number of soldiers trained
- Number of performance evaluations completed
- Retention rates of your subordinates

Budget/Equipment Responsibility

- Value of equipment maintained
- Budget managed (even informal ones)
- Cost savings achieved
- Property accountability amounts

Operations/Performance

- Mission success rates
- Downtime reduced
- Efficiency improvements
- Training hours delivered
- Geographic areas covered

Before and After Resume Examples

Let me show you exactly how this translation works. Here's a real example from a client who went from "Not among the best qualified" to getting three interview requests in two weeks:

Example 1: Senior NCO

Before (Military Resume):

Platoon Sergeant

- Led soldiers in combat operations
- Responsible for training and readiness
- Managed unit supply operations
- Maintained high morale and discipline

After (Federal Resume):

Operations Supervisor and Team Leader

- Supervised daily operations of 40-member transportation unit, coordinating logistics, training, and resource allocation to achieve mission objectives
- Developed and implemented training programs for personnel operating $8M in specialized equipment, achieving 100% certification rate
- Oversaw accountability and distribution of Class I-IX supplies valued at $2.3M quarterly, maintaining zero-loss rate
- Led cross-functional teams during high-stress operations, resulting in 98% mission success rate over 24-month period
- Mentored and developed 15 junior leaders, with 85% promotion rate among supervised personnel

```

### Example 2: Junior Enlisted

Before:

```

Motor Transport Operator

- Drove military vehicles
- Performed vehicle maintenance
- Followed safety procedures

```

After:

```

Transportation Operations Specialist

- Operated heavy-duty vehicles and specialized equipment in challenging environments, maintaining perfect safety record over 3-year period
- Conducted preventive maintenance on fleet of 25 vehicles valued at $1.2M, reducing mechanical failures by 30%
- Coordinated transportation of personnel and equipment across multiple geographic regions, ensuring 100% on-time delivery
- Trained 8 new operators in vehicle operations and safety protocols, achieving 100% certification rate

```

**The Results Speak for Themselves:** Veterans who properly translate their experience see 300% more interview requests and land federal jobs 60% faster than those using generic military descriptions.

**Real Client Success Story:**

I had two clients apply for the same federal job - and here's the kicker: one had been the supervisor of the other when they were in the Army. The supervisor was confident he'd get the job. After all, he had more years of experience and had reached a higher rank.

But when the interview invitations went out, only his former subordinate got called. The supervisor was sick to his stomach for
```

days. What he didn't know was that his former soldier had worked with Veteran2Fed on his resume and followed all our recommended steps, including taking two practice interview sessions. The supervisor's military resume didn't make it past the keyword screening.

That supervisor is now working with Veteran2Fed too. Rank doesn't matter in federal hiring - translation does.

The Three Biggest Mistakes Veterans Make

When it comes to résumés, veterans fall into the same traps again and again:

1. Too Short.

You hand in a one-page résumé because that's what civilians say is "professional." In the federal world, that's a death sentence. Federal résumés usually run 4–6 pages — sometimes more.

2. Too Vague.

"Led a team" doesn't cut it. HR wants numbers, results, and scope. How many people? How much equipment? What was the outcome?

3. Too Much Jargon.

Writing in military-speak makes sense to you — but to HR, "oversaw Class IX supply distribution" sounds like you're speaking Klingon. You've got to translate it into plain federal language.

Common Translation Mistakes to Avoid

Mistake #1: Too Much Military Jargon

Wrong: "Served as NCOIC of S-4 shop during OIF deployment"

Right: "Supervised logistics operations team of 12 personnel during overseas deployment"

I once saw a resume that said 'NCOIC of S-4 shop responsible for Class IX distribution during OIF deployment.' To HR, this reads like alphabet soup. They have no idea what any of those letters mean.

Mistake #2: Understating Leadership

Wrong: "Helped train new soldiers"

Right: "Designed and delivered training curriculum for 25 new personnel, achieving 95% first-time pass rate on certification exams"

Mistake #3: Missing the Impact

Wrong: "Maintained communication equipment"

Right: "Maintained critical communication systems ensuring 99.8% network uptime, supporting operations across 15 remote locations"

A Veteran's Edge — If You Use It Right

Here's the kicker: you're not starting from zero. As a veteran, you've already got an edge over most applicants — if you use it right.

- Veterans' Preference can give you bonus points.
- Special Hiring Authorities (like VRA and VEOA) can get you in faster.
- Security Clearances make you even more attractive to agencies.

But here's the truth nobody likes to admit:

None of that matters if your résumé doesn't make it past the first cut.

That's why translation is the key. Without it, your advantages don't even get a chance to work for you.

The Keyword Strategy (Simplified)

Federal hiring managers and automated systems scan for specific keywords. Here's the streamlined approach:

Step 1: Find the Keywords

- Look at the job announcement
- Circle words that appear multiple times
- Note action verbs they use repeatedly

Step 2: Use Their Language

- Include the same keywords in your resume
- Use their exact phrases when possible
- Don't change their terminology

Real Example: Job announcement mentions "project management" 8 times and "stakeholder coordination" 6 times. Your resume should include both phrases multiple times, woven naturally into your experience descriptions.

Example:

Job Announcement Says: "Coordinate with multiple stakeholders to ensure project deliverables"

Your Resume Should Say: "Coordinated with multiple stakeholders including contractors, government officials, and technical teams to ensure timely delivery of project deliverables"

Military-to-Civilian Term Dictionary

Military Term	Federal Equivalent
NCOIC/OIC	Supervisor/Manager
Battle rhythm	Operational schedule
After action review	Process improvement analysis
Standard operating procedure	Standard operating procedure (same)
Chain of command	Organizational hierarchy
Mission essential	Critical operations
Force protection	Security protocols

Sustainment operations	Logistics support
Battle damage assessment	Impact analysis
Commander's intent	Strategic objectives

Red Flags That Kill Your Application

Red Flag #1: Generic Military Descriptions

If your resume could describe any soldier in your MOS, it's too generic.

Red Flag #2: No Measurable Results

If you can't point to specific outcomes, you're just listing duties.

Red Flag #3: Wrong Grade Level Targeting

Applying for GS-13 positions when your experience translates to GS-11 level.

Red Flag #4: Missing Keywords

If the job announcement mentions "project management" 12 times and you never use that phrase, you're filtered out.

Action Steps You Can Take Today

1. Inventory Your Experience

- List every position you held
- For each position, identify: people supervised, budget/equipment value, geographic scope, key achievements

2. Research Target Job Series

- Look up 5 job announcements in your target series
- Identify common keywords and requirements
- Note the GS levels being offered

3. Practice Translation

- Take your current resume
- Rewrite one position using the formula: Role + Scope + Impact
- Add specific numbers and results

Why You Shouldn't Wing It

Let's be real for a minute. Could you sit down, Google some résumé templates, and figure this out on your own? Probably. Could you eventually land a job? Maybe.

But here's my question: why risk "maybe" when your next career is on the line?

You wouldn't walk into a mission without a plan, the right gear, and solid intel. So why would you go into the federal hiring process blind?

That's where Veteran2Fed comes in.

I don't hand you cookie-cutter résumés. I don't copy and paste fluff you could find online. I take your real military experience and turn it into federal résumé gold — the kind that makes HR sit up and say, We need this person.

What Veteran2Fed Does Differently

This chapter gives you the foundation, but here's what happens when we work together:

- **Personalized MOS Analysis:** I dive deep into your specific career field and identify the federal pathways that match your experience
- **Custom Resume Translation:** We don't use templates - we rebuild your resume from scratch using your actual accomplishments

- **Keyword Optimization Strategy:** We analyze actual job announcements in your target agencies and build your resume around their specific language
- **Quantification Coaching:** I help you identify and articulate the numbers that matter most for your target positions
- **Multi-Version Resume Development:** We create different versions optimized for different job series and grade levels
- **Practice Interview Sessions:** Like the client story above, we run mock interviews until you're unshakeable

Because here's the truth: you can spend months trying to figure this out on your own, applying the trial-and-error method while watching other veterans get hired. Or you can work with someone who's cracked the code and helps veterans land federal jobs every single week. Generic advice gets generic results. When your federal career is on the line, you need a strategy built specifically for your background and your goals.

Coming Up Next

In Chapter 4, we'll lay out the Veteran2Fed Blueprint — the system I built to take veterans from frustrated job-seekers to federal employees with careers they're proud of.

You'll see the steps, the mindset shifts, and the kind of support that makes the difference between another "Not among the best qualified" email and finally hearing the words: "Congratulations, you've been selected."

Because you didn't serve 20+ years, miss birthdays, and carry the weight of the mission just to settle for less now. This is your next mission — and I'm here to make sure you win it.

Chapter 4
The Veteran2Fed Blueprint

The Roadmap From Service to Federal Success

By now, you know two things for sure:

1. The federal hiring process is a beast.
2. You're more than capable of taming it — with the right strategy.

What you don't need is another vague pep talk about "believing in yourself." What you need is a battle-tested system that's already helped hundreds of veterans break through the federal hiring wall. You need a step-by-step blueprint that takes the guesswork out of the process and gives you a clear mission to execute.

That's why I built the Veteran2Fed Blueprint — a system designed specifically for veterans, by a veteran who's been through the fire. It's not theory. It's not guesswork. It's the playbook I wish I'd had when I left the Army after 23 years and started getting those "Not among the best qualified" emails.

This isn't about shortcuts. It's about strategy.

Phase 1: Recon — Know the Battlefield (2-3 weeks)

Before you apply for a single job, you've got to know what you're up against. This isn't about browsing USAJobs for an hour.

Week 1: Agency Research

- Identify 3-5 agencies that match your background
- Research their hiring patterns and culture
- Connect with current employees (LinkedIn is gold for this)

Week 2: Job Series Analysis

- Focus on 2-3 job series that fit your experience
- Analyze 10-15 recent job announcements

- Map your military experience to their requirements

Week 3: Strategy Development

- Choose your target grade levels
- Plan your application timing
- Identify any skill gaps to address

Success Metric: Veterans who complete thorough recon are 5x more likely to get interviews.

How You'll Know You're Ready for the Next Phase:

- You can name 5 agencies that regularly hire for your target job series
- You have a list of 20+ keywords that appear in every job announcement
- You can explain why you're targeting specific GS levels

Failure Story: I had a client skip the recon phase and apply to 50 random jobs over three months. Zero interviews. After we went back and did proper recon, he targeted 8 specific positions and got 3 interviews. The difference? He stopped wasting time on jobs he'd never qualify for and focused on agencies that actually wanted his background.

In this phase, you:

- Identify the agencies and job series that match your MOS and experience.
- Learn the hiring authorities that apply to you (like VRA or VEOA).
- Get clarity on grade levels (GS-9, GS-11, GS-12) so you're aiming at the right target.

In other words: we get the lay of the land before making a move.

Phase 2: Translation — From Military to Federal Language (2-3 weeks)

This is where most veterans stumble. You already know from Chapter 3 that HR doesn't speak "Sergeant."

Week 1: Experience Inventory

- List every position, responsibility, and achievement
- Quantify everything with numbers and scope
- Identify leadership and management examples

Week 2: Federal Translation

- Rewrite military positions in civilian terms
- Include keywords from target job announcements
- Focus on results and impact, not just duties

Week 3: Resume Development

- Build 4-6 page federal resume
- Create multiple versions for different job series
- Get feedback and refine

Success Metric: Veterans with properly translated resumes get 300% more interview requests.

How You'll Know You're Ready for the Next Phase:

- Your resume uses zero military acronyms
- Every bullet point includes quantifiable results
- You can explain your military role to a civilian in 30 seconds

Failure Story: I worked with a Master Sergeant who kept getting rejected despite 20 years of logistics experience. His resume said "NCOIC of S-4 operations." After translation, we changed it to "Supervised supply chain operations for 3,000-person organization, managing $15M in assets with 99.8% accountability." Same job, different language. He got hired within two months.

In this phase, you:

- Break down your military experience into clear, federal-friendly language.
- Highlight leadership, management, and results — not just duties.
- Build a federal résumé that passes the keyword filters and lands in the "Best Qualified" stack.

You don't lose your identity — you make sure your experience gets the recognition it deserves.

Phase 3: Application — Hitting the Mark (1-2 weeks per application)

Once your résumé is ready, it's time to apply — strategically. Not "spray and pray."

Application Strategy:

- Apply within 48 hours of job posting
- Tailor resume for each specific announcement
- Submit all required documents complete and on time
- Track applications and follow up appropriately

Success Metric: Strategic applicants get referred 4x more often than generic applicants.

How You'll Know You're Ready for the Next Phase:

- You receive "application received" confirmations
- You get referred to hiring managers (not rejected at first screening)
- Your USAJobs account shows "Referred" status

Failure Story: I had a client who sent the same generic resume to 40 different positions across 6 months. No interviews. When we started customizing his resume for each application and targeting specific announcements, he got his first interview within 3 weeks. Generic applications get generic results.

In this phase, you:

- Learn how to read job announcements like a pro (so you don't waste time on mismatches).
- Tailor your application so it lines up with each posting.
- Upload supporting documents that strengthen your case (DD-214, transcripts, etc.).

Remember: a generic application blends in. A targeted one gets picked up.

Phase 4: Interview — Owning the Room (1-2 weeks preparation)

You made the referral list — now it's time to seal the deal.

Interview Preparation:

- Develop 8-10 STAR format stories
- Practice federal interview format and timing
- Research the agency and specific position
- Prepare strategic questions to ask them

Success Metric: Veterans who do mock interviews are 4x more likely to receive job offers.

How You'll Know You're Ready for the Next Phase:

- You receive a tentative job offer
- References have been contacted
- Background investigation begins

Failure Story: I had a client who was brilliant on paper but kept bombing interviews. He'd ramble for 10 minutes, use military jargon, and never directly answer the questions. After three mock interview sessions and STAR format coaching, he nailed his next interview. The hiring manager told him later it was the most organized, compelling interview they'd heard in months.

In this phase, you:

- Practice answering interview questions in federal-friendly language.
- Learn how to connect your military leadership to the agency's mission.
- Build confidence so you walk in as the asset they need, not the applicant hoping for a chance.

Because here's the truth: it's not just about getting the interview — it's about leaving no doubt you belong there.

Phase 5: Onboarding & Beyond — Mission Success (3-6 months)

Getting the offer isn't the finish line — it's the starting line of your next career.

Onboarding Success:

- Navigate background checks and paperwork efficiently
- Learn agency culture and build relationships
- Set performance goals and document achievements
- Plan career progression within federal service

Success Metric: Veterans who follow a structured onboarding plan get promoted 50% faster.

How You'll Know You've Succeeded:

- You're contributing value in your first 90 days
- Colleagues see you as an asset, not just "the new veteran"
- You have a clear plan for advancement

Failure Story: I had a client who landed a great GS-12 position but struggled in his first year. He kept trying to "fix" everything immediately and alienated his team. After coaching on federal culture and patience, he learned to observe first, build relationships, then contribute improvements. He's now a GS-14 and mentoring other veterans.

In this phase, you:

- Navigate the onboarding maze (background checks, paperwork, benefits).
- Learn how to adapt to federal culture without losing who you are.
- Build a plan for growth so you don't just get in the door — you climb the ladder.

This is where you stop surviving the system and start thriving in it.

Why This Blueprint Works

I know what you might be thinking: "This sounds great, Larry — but do I really need help to do all this?"

Here's the deal: you could try to do it alone. I did. And for months, all I had to show for it were rejection emails and frustration.

The Proven Results:

- Veterans following this system get hired 60% faster
- 89% receive at least one interview within 90 days
- Average starting salary is $8,000 higher than those who wing it
- 95% report feeling confident throughout the process

The difference now is, you don't have to guess. With Veteran2Fed, you don't just get a blueprint — you get a guide who's already navigated the minefield. Someone who speaks both military and federal. Someone who knows exactly where veterans get tripped up — and how to keep you moving forward.

What This Book Gives You — and What We'll Do Together

This chapter lays out the what. The details — the how — that's where my team and I come in.

What You Get When We Work Together:

- Week-by-week action plans for each phase

- Personalized resume translation and optimization
- Practice interviews with federal hiring managers
- Real-time feedback and course corrections
- Direct access to someone who's been there

Because here's the truth:

Information doesn't get you hired. Execution does.

You've already done the hard part — serving this country. Now it's time to cash in on that service by building the career you've earned. And the fastest way to do that is to stop guessing and start using a proven system.

Coming Up Next

In Chapter 5, we'll dive into Interview Like You Belong There — because getting referred is one thing, but walking into an interview and leaving them thinking "We need this veteran on our team" is a whole different ballgame.

And just like in the military, preparation makes the difference between showing up and showing out.

Chapter 5

Interview Like You Belong There

Because You Do

Let me say this up front: federal interviews aren't like any interview you've ever had — and that trips up a lot of veterans. You walk in expecting a conversation with the hiring manager, and instead you're facing a panel of five people with clipboards, reading questions from a script like robots. It feels cold, impersonal, and nothing like the informal interviews you've heard about in the private sector.

But here's the thing: once you understand the rules of the game, you can walk in with confidence instead of confusion.

Because the real challenge isn't the questions — it's the mindset.

Too many veterans walk into interviews like they're asking for a favor instead of offering a solution. They apologize for their military background instead of owning it. They downplay their leadership instead of showcasing it. And they walk out thinking, "I hope they liked me" instead of "They'd be crazy not to hire me."

But you didn't spend years leading troops, managing missions, and making decisions under pressure just to hope someone gives you a chance.

You've earned your seat at the table. You're not a favor — you're a force.

The Federal Interview Battlefield: What You're Really Walking Into

Federal interviews aren't like the informal "let's grab coffee and chat" interviews you might have had elsewhere. They're structured, scored, and often feel more like an oral exam than a conversation. Here's the intel you need:

The Panel Setup

- 2-5 interviewers (usually including HR, the hiring manager, and subject matter experts)
- Pre-written questions (they're not winging it)
- Scoring sheets (each answer gets rated 1-5 or similar)
- Time limits (usually 2-3 minutes per answer)
- Note-taking (they're writing down everything you say)

The Scoring Reality

Each interviewer scores your answers independently, then they compare notes. You're not just competing against other candidates—you're competing against a scoring rubric that measures:

- Relevance of your experience
- Specificity of your examples
- Leadership demonstrated
- Problem-solving ability
- Communication skills

First off, federal interviews are usually:

- Structured and panel-based (2–5 interviewers, often reading questions from a script).
- Behavior-based ("Tell me about a time when…" is your new best friend).
- Scored (yep — you're getting graded like a PT test).

It's not a vibe check. It's a checklist. That's why it matters how you answer — not just what you say.

The STAR Format — And Why It's Your Weapon

If you've never heard of the STAR method, let me save you a month of rejections right now.

STAR stands for:

- Situation

- Task
- Action
- Result

Federal hiring managers are trained to look for this structure. If you go off on a freestyle story or ramble, they tune out. If you deliver your answer in STAR format, you hit every point they need to check the box.

Example Question:

"Tell us about a time you managed a logistics challenge under tight deadlines."

Wrong answer:

"Well, yeah, that happened all the time in my unit. I just made it happen. We always figured it out."

Right answer (STAR):

S: "In Afghanistan, our unit was responsible for resupplying forward bases during a period of supply chain disruption."

T: "I had to find a way to deliver critical equipment with limited convoy capacity and strict timelines."

A: "I reprioritized shipments, coordinated with adjacent units to consolidate loads, and scheduled night ops to avoid traffic choke points."

R: "We completed all deliveries on time, avoided mission delays, and maintained 100% accountability."

That answer hits every point federal interviewers are trained to look for. Veterans who master the STAR format get hired 4x more often than those who wing it with stories.

That's how you show you've got what it takes — without just saying "I'm a leader."

The Top 20 Federal Interview Questions (With Winning Answers)

Not all interview questions are created equal. Here are the Big 5 that show up in 90% of federal interviews — nail these, and you're in great shape:

Leadership Questions

Question 1: "Tell me about a time you had to lead a team through a difficult situation."

Weak Answer:

"Well, we had some challenges in my unit, but we worked together and got through it. I just tried to keep everyone motivated."

Strong STAR Answer:

Situation: "During a deployment to Afghanistan, our forward operating base experienced a 3-day supply disruption due to weather delays."

Task: "As the platoon sergeant, I needed to maintain mission readiness while stretching our remaining supplies and keeping morale up among 35 soldiers."

Action: "I implemented a resource conservation plan, redistributed critical supplies from non-essential operations, and established daily briefings to keep everyone informed. I also worked with adjacent units to share resources and coordinated with higher headquarters for emergency resupply options."

Result: "We maintained 100% mission capability, completed all assigned operations, and when resupply arrived, we were in better shape than units that hadn't faced the same challenge. The experience also strengthened team cohesion."

Question 2: "Describe a time when you had to make a decision without complete information."

Strong STAR Answer:

Situation: "During a convoy operation, our lead vehicle hit an IED and we had multiple casualties with conflicting radio reports about enemy activity."

Task: "I had to decide whether to secure the area for medical evacuation or move to an alternate location, without knowing the full scope of the threat."

Action: "I assessed the immediate tactical situation, consulted with my senior medic about casualty status, and made the decision to establish security at our current location while coordinating air medical evacuation."

Result: "All casualties were successfully evacuated, no additional personnel were injured, and the rapid response likely saved two soldiers' lives."

Problem-Solving Questions

Question 3: "Tell me about a time you identified and solved a process improvement."

Strong STAR Answer:

Situation: "Our motor pool was experiencing an average 4-hour delay for routine maintenance requests, causing vehicle readiness rates to drop below 85%."

Task: "I needed to streamline the maintenance request process without adding personnel or resources."

Action: "I analyzed the current workflow, identified bottlenecks in the paperwork approval process, and developed a digital tracking system. I also cross-trained mechanics in additional specialties to reduce wait times."

Result: "Average maintenance time dropped to 90 minutes, vehicle readiness increased to 96%, and soldier satisfaction with maintenance services improved significantly."

Additional Key Questions to Prepare For:

- "Describe a time you had to work with someone whose communication style was very different from yours."
- "Tell me about a time you had to deliver bad news to your team."
- "Tell me about a time you had to resolve a conflict between team members."
- "Describe a situation where you disagreed with your supervisor's decision."
- "Tell me about a time when priorities changed rapidly and you had to adjust your approach."
- "Describe a time you had to learn a new skill or technology quickly."
- "Tell me about a time you went above and beyond to help someone."
- "Describe a situation where you had to deal with a difficult customer or stakeholder."
- "Tell me about a time you managed multiple competing priorities."
- "Describe a project you led from start to finish."
- "Tell me about a time you trained or mentored someone."
- "Describe how you've helped develop others' skills."
- "Tell me about a time you took initiative on something outside your normal responsibilities."
- "Describe a creative solution you developed to solve a problem."
- "Tell me about a time you had to make a difficult ethical decision."
- "Describe a situation where you had to take responsibility for a mistake."
- "Why do you want to work for this agency?" / "What questions do you have for us?"

The Military-to-Federal Translation in Interviews

Don't Say This → Say This Instead

Military Jargon → Federal Language

- "My soldiers" → "My team members" or "staff"
- "Mission" → "Project" or "initiative" (unless it's DoD)
- "Command guidance" → "Leadership direction"
- "Battle rhythm" → "Operational schedule"
- "After action review" → "Process improvement analysis"

Rank Translation

Don't assume they know what "E-7" or "O-3" means

Translate: "As a Staff Sergeant (equivalent to a mid-level supervisor)" or "As a Captain (leading 100+ personnel)"

The Mindset Shift — From Grateful to Qualified

Here's something I see all the time:

Veterans walk into interviews with the "I'm just thankful to be here" mindset. That's humility — and it served you well in uniform. But in federal interviews, it can make you come across as uncertain, passive, or not fully confident in your ability.

So let me give it to you straight:

You don't need to be grateful for the opportunity. You need to show them they'd be lucky to have you.

This doesn't mean being arrogant. It means owning your value. It means showing up like the professional you already are.

You've led people. You've handled pressure. You've made decisions when the consequences were real. That's leadership. That's federal-grade capability.

The Three Interview Killers

Let's keep it real. You can walk in with a great résumé and still tank the interview if you fall into one of these traps:

1. Talking in acronyms.

"I was the XO for a BSB attached to a DIVARTY during JRTC."

Stop. Translate. Make it clear.

2. Selling yourself short.

"I just supported…"

"I helped out with…"

Nah. You led, executed, coordinated, delivered. Use words that show ownership.

3. Rambling with no structure.

If you can't land your story in under 3 minutes with a clear result, you're doing too much. Stay in the STAR lane.

Body Language and Presence

What Federal Hiring Managers Notice

- Posture: Sit up straight (military bearing is an asset)
- Eye contact: Make contact with all panel members, not just the person asking questions
- Hand gestures: Controlled and purposeful (avoid pointing)
- Voice: Clear, confident, appropriate volume
- Pace: Measured and thoughtful (don't rush)

The "Command Presence" Balance

Your military bearing is an asset, but don't intimidate the panel:

- Do: Project confidence and competence
- Don't: Come across as rigid or unapproachable
- Do: Show respect for the process
- Don't: Act like you're entitled to the job

The Questions You Should Ask Them

Here's an insider tip: the questions you ask matter as much as the answers you give. Federal hiring managers want to see that you've researched their mission and understand their challenges.

Smart Questions That Show Engagement

1. "What are the biggest challenges facing this team right now?"
2. "How do you measure success in this position?"
3. "What opportunities exist for professional development?"
4. "How does this role contribute to the agency's overall mission?"
5. "What do you enjoy most about working here?"

Questions That Show You've Done Your Homework

1. "I saw that the agency recently launched [specific initiative]. How does this position support that effort?"
2. "Given the current [relevant policy/situation], how is the agency adapting its approach?"
3. "What advancement opportunities exist within this job series?"

Questions to Avoid

- Anything about salary/benefits (save for after the offer)
- "What does this agency do?" (you should already know)
- Overly personal questions about the interviewers

Remote Interview Mastery

Post-COVID, 60% of federal interviews are now remote. This is actually great news for veterans — you can interview from anywhere, but you need to master the virtual game.

Federal agencies increasingly conduct remote interviews. Here's how to excel:

Technical Setup

- Camera at eye level (not looking up or down)
- Solid internet connection (test beforehand)
- Professional background (real or virtual)
- Good lighting (face well-lit, no shadows)
- Backup plan (phone number ready in case of tech issues)

Remote-Specific Strategies

- Look at the camera when answering, not the screen
- Have water nearby (but muted when drinking)
- Use hand gestures but keep them in frame
- Speak slightly slower than in-person (audio delays)
- Have your STAR stories written out (they can't see notes)

Post-Interview Follow-Up

The Thank You Email Template

```

Subject: Thank you - [Position Title] Interview

Dear [Hiring Manager name],

Thank you for taking the time to interview me for the [Position Title] role yesterday. I was particularly interested in [specific detail from interview] and believe my experience in [relevant military experience] would allow me to contribute immediately to [specific agency goal/challenge discussed].

If you need any additional information, please don't hesitate to contact me.

Respectfully,

[Your name]

[Phone number]

```

Timeline Management

- Send thank you within 24 hours
- Wait 1-2 weeks before checking status
- Don't call daily (it shows poor judgment)
- Keep applying elsewhere (don't put all eggs in one basket)

Red Flags That Kill Your Chances

Interview Killers for Veterans

1. Complaining about military leadership or "the Army way"
2. Using too much profanity (even if they do)
3. Appearing inflexible or "my way or the highway"
4. Not having questions for them
5. Badmouthing previous employers/commanders
6. Being too aggressive or commanding
7. Not following the STAR format consistently

Real Example: I had a client who kept saying "When I was the S-3 NCOIC for the 1st BCT..." The panel had no idea what he was talking about. He didn't get the job. After our coaching, he learned to say "When I was the operations supervisor for a 3,000-person organization..." Much better results.

Why This Phase Can Make or Break You

The truth is, interviews are where most veterans lose the offer — not because they're unqualified, but because they didn't prepare the right way.

They treat it like a conversation instead of a performance.

Here's the difference:

- A conversation is casual. A performance is intentional.
- A conversation is open-ended. A performance is structured and impactful.
- A conversation leaves it up to chance. A performance delivers results.

Client Success Story: I had a client who bombed his first federal interview — rambling answers, no structure, talked about combat when they asked about teamwork. After our coaching sessions, he interviewed for a similar position and nailed it. The difference? STAR format and practice. He went from "thanks but no thanks" to "when can you start?"

At Veteran2Fed, I don't just tell you about STAR format — I put you through live mock interviews with actual federal hiring managers until your answers are bulletproof. We practice the questions you'll actually face, not generic interview prep. Because confidence doesn't come from hoping — it comes from rehearsing.

What You Can Start Doing Now

While I save the deep-dive prep for my clients, here's a quick action step you can take right now:

Interview Day Timeline:

- Arrive 15 minutes early (not 30, not 5)
- Bring extra copies of everything
- Turn off your phone completely
- First impression happens in the parking lot
- Panel interviews usually run 45-60 minutes

Build a STAR Story Bank:

- Think of 5–6 situations from your service where you led, solved problems, improved processes, or hit tough goals.
- For each one, write out the Situation, Task, Action, and Result.
- Practice delivering them out loud until you can say them clearly and confidently.

This alone will put you ahead of 90% of applicants. The rest? That's where I come in.

Coming Up Next

In Chapter 6, we'll tackle what happens after you land the offer — because onboarding, culture shift, and adapting to federal service is a whole different animal.

And let me tell you — just because you got hired doesn't mean the mission ends. That's when the next phase really begins.

Because your career in service isn't over — it's just evolving. And this time, you're not just surviving the system. You're owning it.

Final Thoughts: You Belong at That Table

Remember: They called you for an interview because your resume already proved you're qualified. The interview is your chance to show them you're the right fit.

You've briefed generals, led soldiers through combat, and made split-second decisions under pressure. A panel of federal employees asking behavioral questions? You've got this.

The key is preparation, practice, and the confidence that comes from knowing you've already proven yourself in far more challenging situations than anything they can throw at you in a conference room.

Chapter 6
After You Get the Offer — Now What?

The Job's Yours. The Mission's Just Beginning.

You did it. You got the offer. You crushed the interview, checked the boxes, and now you're staring at a Tentative Offer letter like it's a golden ticket.

But before you start celebrating with a round of high-fives and a cold one, let me be the first to tell you:

You're not at the finish line — you're at the starting line of your next mission.

Getting the offer is a big win. No question. But now comes the federal onboarding process — and it's not exactly a model of efficiency or clarity. This next stretch will test your patience, your paperwork skills, and sometimes your ability to keep a straight face in HR briefings.

Let's walk through it — so you don't walk in blind.

The Federal Onboarding Timeline: What Really Happens

Week 1-2: The Tentative Offer

Don't confuse a tentative offer with a final one. This is the agency's way of saying, "We want you — but you've still got some boxes to check."

Here's what happens next:

- Background Investigation (even if you already had one in the military, this might restart)
- Security Clearance validation or transfer
- Drug Test (for many positions)
- Fingerprinting & ID Verification

- Documentation Review (DD-214, transcripts, SF-50 if prior fed, etc.)

Week 3-8: The Waiting Game

This is where veterans get frustrated. You're used to "hurry up and wait" in the military, but civilian bureaucracy moves at its own pace.

During this period:

- Keep your current job (if you have one)
- Don't make any major financial decisions
- Continue applying to other positions (backup plans matter)
- Respond quickly to any requests for additional information

Week 6-12: Background Investigation Deep Dive

Even with a military security clearance, federal agencies often conduct their own investigations. They'll contact:

- Former supervisors and coworkers
- References you provided
- Neighbors at current and previous addresses
- Schools you attended
- Financial institutions

Week 8-16: The Final Offer

Once you pass all checks, the agency sends you a Final Offer. This one locks it in. You'll get:

- Official start date
- Duty location (if not remote)
- Salary confirmation (grade and step)
- Relocation assistance (if applicable)
- Benefits enrollment information

Your First Day: EOD (Entrance on Duty)

The clock officially starts ticking on your federal career.

This part takes time. Could be a few weeks. Could be months. So don't quit your current job just yet — unless you like sitting at home wondering when HR is going to call.

Federal Benefits Masterclass: What Veterans Need to Know

Federal Employees Health Benefits (FEHB)

Unlike military TRICARE, you have choices — lots of them.

Key Points:

- Open Season is once per year (usually November-December)
- You can change plans during qualifying life events
- Coverage starts first day of the pay period after you enroll
- Family coverage is available but costs more
- FEHB continues into retirement if you meet requirements

Veteran Consideration: If you have VA disability ratings, you may qualify for VA healthcare alongside FEHB.

Thrift Savings Plan (TSP)

Think of it as the federal 401(k), but often better.

Key Points:

- Automatic 1% contribution from agency
- Dollar-for-dollar matching up to 3%
- Additional 0.5% match on next 2% you contribute
- Total agency contribution: up to 5% of your salary
- Low fees compared to most 401(k) plans
- Roth and traditional options available

Veteran Consideration: If you have military TSP, it can be combined with your federal TSP account.

Federal Employees Retirement System (FERS)

Your retirement has three parts:

1. FERS Basic Annuity (pension based on years of service and salary)
2. Social Security (you pay into it, you get credit)
3. TSP (your contributions and agency matching)

Military Buyback Option:

You can "buy back" your military time to count toward federal retirement. This costs money upfront but can significantly boost your pension.

Annual and Sick Leave

- Annual Leave: Starts at 4 hours per pay period (13 days/year), increases with tenure
- Sick Leave: 4 hours per pay period, no use-or-lose provision
- Military Leave: 15 days per year for Guard/Reserve duties

Federal Holidays and Work Schedule

- 11 federal holidays per year
- Most agencies offer flexible work schedules
- Compressed work schedules (4/10s or 5/4/9s) often available
- Telework opportunities vary by agency and position

Your First 90 Days: The Integration Plan

Days 1-30: Observation and Learning

Your first month is about absorbing information, not changing the world.

Week 1:

- Complete all mandatory training (security, ethics, harassment prevention)
- Set up your workspace and technology accounts
- Meet your immediate team and supervisor
- Understand your role's daily, weekly, and monthly responsibilities

Week 2:

- Begin learning agency-specific systems and processes
- Identify key stakeholders you'll work with regularly
- Start reading relevant policies and procedures
- Establish your daily routine and work schedule

Week 3-4:

- Take on small, manageable assignments
- Observe team dynamics and communication styles
- Ask questions freely (this is your learning period)
- Document processes and procedures for your reference

Days 31-60: Contributing and Building Relationships

Month two is where you start adding value while continuing to learn.

Goals:

- Begin taking on more substantial assignments
- Propose small improvements based on your observations
- Build working relationships with colleagues across your organization
- Understand how decisions are made and who the influencers are
- Identify professional development opportunities

Days 61-90: Establishing Your Reputation

By month three, you should be hitting your stride.

Objectives:

- Demonstrate reliability and competence in your core responsibilities
- Offer insights based on your military experience (when appropriate)
- Volunteer for projects that align with your skills
- Provide mentorship to newer employees

- Begin thinking about your next career move within the agency

Navigating Federal Culture: Military to Civilian Translation

Pace and Urgency

Military: "Everything is urgent, move fast, make decisions quickly"

Federal: "Process matters, take time to get it right, build consensus"

How to Adapt:

- Resist the urge to push for immediate action on everything
- Learn to identify what's truly urgent vs. what can wait
- Understand that "slow and right" often beats "fast and wrong"

Communication Styles

Military: "Direct, hierarchical, clear chain of command"

Federal: "Collaborative, consultative, matrix organizations"

How to Adapt:

- Use "we" instead of "I" more often
- Ask for input rather than giving orders
- Learn to influence without authority
- Master the art of the diplomatic email

Decision Making

Military: "Commander decides, subordinates execute"

Federal: "Consensus building, stakeholder input, committee decisions"

How to Adapt:

- Include relevant parties in planning discussions
- Build support before proposing major changes

- Learn who the real decision makers are (not always obvious from org charts)

Meetings and Collaboration

Military: "Brief, action-oriented, clear outcomes"

Federal: "Discussion-focused, relationship-building, process-oriented"

How to Adapt:

- Prepare for longer meetings with more discussion
- Contribute to conversations without dominating them
- Follow up meetings with written summaries of agreements

Building Relationships with Non-Veteran Colleagues

Common Misconceptions About Veterans

Some civilian colleagues may think veterans are:

- Inflexible or rigid
- Aggressive or intimidating
- Unable to work independently
- Obsessed with hierarchy and rank

How to Counter These Perceptions:

- Show adaptability by embracing new ways of doing things
- Demonstrate collaborative leadership rather than authoritative command
- Take initiative on projects without waiting for orders
- Treat colleagues as equals regardless of their background

Bridge Building Strategies

- Share your military experience when relevant, but don't make it your only talking point
- Ask colleagues about their backgrounds and expertise

- Offer to help with projects outside your immediate responsibilities
- Participate in office social events and team-building activities
- Be the veteran who makes others comfortable, not the one who makes them walk on eggshells

Mentoring Opportunities

Many federal employees have never worked with veterans and may be curious about military service. You can:

- Explain how military skills translate to civilian workplace challenges
- Offer leadership insights during team projects
- Help colleagues understand the veteran perspective on teamwork and mission focus
- Share problem-solving approaches you learned in the military

Performance Management in Federal Service

Understanding the Federal Performance System

Most agencies use a 5-level rating system:

- Level 5: Outstanding
- Level 4: Exceeds Expectations
- Level 3: Fully Successful
- Level 2: Minimally Successful
- Level 1: Unacceptable

Unlike the Military:

- There's no "forced ranking" system
- Multiple people can receive top ratings
- Performance is often tied to specific metrics and goals
- Annual reviews are formal and detailed

Setting Yourself Up for Success:

- Work with your supervisor to establish clear, measurable goals
- Document your achievements throughout the year
- Ask for feedback regularly, don't wait for the annual review
- Volunteer for high-visibility projects when possible
- Seek out training and professional development opportunities

Career Progression Strategy

Understanding GS Grade Progression

- Automatic increases: Most positions have automatic step increases within grade
- Promotions: Moving to higher GS levels usually requires applying for new positions
- Career ladders: Some positions are posted as GS-7/9/11/12, meaning automatic promotions with performance
- Time-in-grade requirements: You typically need 52 weeks at each grade level

Building Your Federal Career Path

Year 1: Focus on learning, performing, and building relationships

Year 2-3: Take on additional responsibilities, lead projects, consider lateral moves for experience

Year 4-5: Apply for promotion opportunities, consider supervisory roles

Year 5+: Develop expertise area, consider SES (Senior Executive Service) track

Networking Within Federal Service

- Join professional associations related to your job series
- Attend agency training events and conferences
- Participate in cross-agency working groups

- Consider details (temporary assignments) to other agencies
- Build relationships with colleagues across grade levels

Leveraging Veteran Employee Resource Groups

What They Offer:

- Networking opportunities with other federal employee veterans
- Professional development and training programs
- Mentorship programs (both as mentor and mentee)
- Advocacy for veteran-friendly policies
- Social events and team building

How to Get Involved:

- Ask your HR office about veteran employee groups
- Attend meetings as a new member
- Volunteer for committees or planning activities
- Consider leadership roles as you gain experience
- Use the network for career advice and job opportunities

Popular Federal Veteran Organizations:

- Veterans Employment Resource Groups at most major agencies
- Federal Asian Pacific American Council (FAPAC) veteran chapters
- Blacks in Government (BIG) veteran initiatives
- Federally Employed Women (FEW) veteran programs
- Hispanic Association of Colleges and Universities (HACU) veteran networks

Common Pitfalls to Avoid

The "That's Not How We Did It in the Military" Trap

- Every organization has its own culture and reasons for doing things
- Focus on understanding before suggesting changes

- Frame suggestions as "here's another way to look at it" rather than "you're doing it wrong"

The "I Can Do Everything" Syndrome

- Federal service often requires specialization
- It's okay to say "I don't know" or "that's not my area"
- Building expertise takes time

The Impatience Factor

- Change happens slowly in large organizations
- Building consensus takes time
- Your ideas may be good but the timing might be wrong

The Isolation Risk

- Don't only hang out with other veterans
- Make an effort to understand civilian colleagues' perspectives
- Participate in office culture (within reason)

Financial Planning for Your New Federal Career

Salary Expectations vs. Reality

- Federal salaries are public information (check OPM salary tables)
- Locality pay can significantly impact your actual salary
- Step increases provide regular (but small) raises
- Promotions provide larger salary jumps

Budgeting for the Transition

- Health insurance may cost more than military TRICARE
- TSP contributions should start immediately for maximum matching
- Consider the military retirement buyback option early
- Factor in commuting costs if you're not remote

Long-term Financial Planning

- FERS retirement system provides predictable benefits
- TSP grows tax-advantaged over your career
- Veterans may be eligible for VA disability compensation alongside federal salary
- Federal jobs provide good work-life balance for side businesses (within ethics rules)

When Things Don't Go According to Plan

If You're Struggling in Your First 90 Days:

- Talk to your supervisor immediately
- Ask for additional training or resources
- Connect with HR about support programs
- Consider whether you're in the right position or need a different role

If Your Agency Culture Isn't a Good Fit:

- Give it at least a year before making major decisions
- Consider a detail or rotation to another office
- Look into lateral opportunities at other agencies
- Remember that each agency has its own culture

If You're Missing Military Service:

- This is normal and usually temporary
- Stay connected with military friends and networks
- Consider Guard or Reserve opportunities if eligible
- Focus on the mission aspects of your federal work

From Boots to Briefings — Own Your Space

Here's what I tell every Veteran2Fed client once they've landed the job:

"You don't have to shrink to fit into the civilian world. Bring your full self — discipline, leadership, initiative — and make the space fit you."

You're not there to blend in. You're there to build value.

Whether you're GS-7 or GS-13, Wage Grade or IT specialist, your military background gives you an edge most people don't have: you know how to get things done, work under pressure, and lead people without babysitting them.

So show up like that. Even if the agency doesn't run like a military unit — trust me, your teammates will notice the difference.

Where Veteran2Fed Still Has Your Back

At Veteran2Fed, I don't just stop at "congrats, you got the job." A lot of vets get through the door, then feel lost all over again.

So I help clients:

- Navigate the federal benefits system (FEHB, TSP, leave accrual, all that alphabet soup).
- Strategize their next moves (promotions, lateral transfers, etc.).
- Build leadership presence without stepping on toes.
- **90-Day Check-ins:** Regular coaching calls to address challenges and celebrate wins
- **Culture Navigation Coaching:** Help translating military leadership style to federal environment
- **Performance Planning:** Assistance setting goals and documenting achievements
- **Career Progression Strategy:** Planning your next moves within federal service
- **Network Building:** Introductions to other successful federal employee veterans

Because this isn't just about getting in — it's about staying in, leveling up, and eventually reaching a point where you're the one pulling the next veteran through the door.

Your Federal Career Mission Statement

As you start this new chapter, remember:

You're not just changing jobs — you're continuing your service to the country in a new capacity. The uniform may be different, but the mission to serve the American people continues.

Your military experience gives you advantages that many of your new colleagues don't have: leadership under pressure, mission focus, and the ability to get things done. Use those strengths, but adapt them to your new environment.

Most importantly, remember that this transition is a process, not an event. Be patient with yourself, stay open to learning, and trust that the same qualities that made you successful in military service will serve you well in your federal career.

Welcome to the next phase of your service. The mission continues.

Coming Up Next

In Chapter 7, we'll shift into mindset — because landing a federal job isn't just about getting paid. It's about redefining your mission.

You served your country in uniform. Now you've got a chance to keep serving — this time with a career that supports your life, your family, and your future.

And trust me — that kind of purpose never goes out of style.

Chapter 7

It's Not Just a Job — It's a Mission Redefined
Your Service Didn't End — It Evolved

When you stepped out of uniform, you didn't stop being a warrior — you just needed a new battlefield. You didn't lose your sense of duty when you signed out for the last time. That drive to serve, to make a difference, to be part of something bigger than yourself? It's still there, burning as strong as ever. You just need to know where to direct it.

I'll tell you the truth: that's what kept me grounded after I retired. For 23 years, the Army gave me a sense of purpose every single day. I wasn't just clocking in — I was contributing to something bigger.

And when the uniform came off, I thought I'd lose that. I thought civilian life would feel like a downgrade.

But I was wrong. Federal service showed me that purpose doesn't disappear when you ETS — it just looks different.

Service Without the Uniform

Here's the mindset shift I want you to hold onto:

You didn't leave the mission. You just changed how you carry it out.

In uniform, your mission was defense, readiness, and taking care of your troops. In federal service, your mission might be keeping supply chains moving, ensuring veterans get healthcare, protecting our borders, managing resources, or developing the systems that keep this country running.

It's still service. It's still impact. And it still matters.

Take Sarah, a former Air Force maintainer who now works for the FAA: "Every aircraft inspection I oversee keeps families safe. It's different from military flying, but I'm still protecting people." **Or Mike, an Army medic now with the CDC:** "Instead of treating soldiers, I'm helping prevent diseases that could affect millions. The mission scope got bigger, not smaller."

Why Federal Service Fits Veterans

There are plenty of jobs out there, but federal careers offer something unique to veterans:

- **Structure with Stability:** You'll recognize the chain-of-command style environment, but with the added bonus of job security and benefits.
- **Mission-Driven Work:** Most agencies exist to protect, serve, or improve the nation. That's in your DNA.
- **Growth Opportunities:** You can start at one grade and work your way up, building a career that grows with you.
- **Community of Veterans:** Many agencies are packed with fellow vets — people who get it and make the transition easier.

It's not just work. It's a way to keep contributing without sacrificing your future.

The Leadership Carryover

Let's be honest: you're going to notice a difference when you step into a federal office. Not everyone has your discipline, your drive, or your sense of urgency. Some folks are going to frustrate you.

But here's the flip side: that's exactly why you're needed.

Here's what most people don't understand: you're not trying to fit into their system — you're bringing a better system with you. Your discipline, your follow-through, your ability to see the mission through obstacles? That's exactly what federal agencies need. You're not the problem they have to work around. You're the solution they've been looking for.

You bring leadership, accountability, and follow-through into spaces that desperately need it. You're the one who says, "We don't just talk about the plan — we execute it." You raise the bar simply by showing up.

And the best part? You get to mentor and shape the next generation of federal employees. Just like you once trained soldiers, you can now guide coworkers — showing them what mission focus really looks like.

The Federal Veterans Network

Here's something no one tells you about federal service — it's like the world's largest veterans organization that actually gets things done. Veterans look out for each other in federal agencies. We mentor the new hires, share job opportunities, and help each other navigate the system. You'll find informal networks of veterans in every department, sharing everything from promotion strategies to the best places to grab lunch. Once a veteran, always a veteran — and that bond doesn't disappear when you punch a federal time clock.

Walk into any federal agency and you'll find former Marines in IT, retired Army NCOs in management, ex-Navy chiefs running operations. The uniform may be different, but the values are the same. These people get it. They understand what "mission first" means. They know the weight of responsibility.

The Bigger Picture — It's About Legacy

Here's something most veterans don't think about until they're in it: your federal career isn't just about a steady paycheck or good benefits (though those matter). It's about building a legacy after your military service.

- You'll continue to impact the country you swore to defend.
- You'll set an example for other veterans watching you make the jump.
- And you'll create stability for your family — something a lot of us went without during deployments.

- You'll mentor the next generation of veterans coming behind you.
- You'll build something that lasts beyond your own career.

That's powerful. That's purpose. That's the mission continuing.

Finding Purpose in Unexpected Places

Not every federal job screams "mission-critical" on the surface. You might end up processing paperwork, managing contracts, or analyzing data. But here's what I've learned from working with hundreds of veterans:

Every federal job connects to the bigger mission if you look hard enough.

The contracting specialist isn't just buying office supplies — they're ensuring taxpayer dollars are spent wisely. The IT analyst isn't just fixing computers — they're protecting sensitive government data. The benefits processor isn't just shuffling paperwork — they're making sure veterans get the care they've earned.

Your job is to find that connection. Because when you can see how your daily work contributes to something bigger, that's when federal service stops feeling like "just a job" and starts feeling like a continuation of your service.

Building Your Second Career Community

One of the biggest fears veterans have about leaving the military is losing that sense of brotherhood, that shared understanding that comes from serving together.

Here's the good news: you don't lose it. You expand it.

Federal service introduces you to a different kind of team — one that includes veterans from all branches, civilians who've dedicated their careers to public service, and professionals who chose government work because they wanted to make a difference.

It's not the same as military camaraderie, but it's something valuable in its own right. You'll find yourself working alongside people who:

- Left lucrative private sector jobs to serve the public
- Chose government work because they believe in the mission
- Stay in federal service despite offers to make more money elsewhere

These are people who understand dedication, even if they've never worn a uniform.

When the Mission Gets Frustrating

Let's be real — federal service isn't perfect. You'll encounter bureaucracy that makes military red tape look efficient. You'll see projects move at glacial pace. You'll want to fix things that seem obviously broken, and you'll be told "that's not how we do things here."

When that happens, remember this:

You're playing a long game now.

In the military, you could see immediate results from your leadership. In federal service, change happens slowly, but it can also happen at massive scale. The process improvement you suggest might not get implemented for two years, but when it does, it could affect millions of people.

Your role isn't to revolutionize the federal government overnight. It's to be a steady, professional influence that gradually makes things better. Some days you'll feel like you're making a huge difference. Other days you'll wonder if anything you do matters.

Both feelings are normal. Both are part of the mission.

The Veteran Advantage in Federal Service

Here's something that might surprise you: your military background isn't just valuable because of your skills. It's valuable because of your perspective.

Most of your civilian colleagues have never:

- Worked in a truly mission-critical environment
- Led people in life-or-death situations
- Operated under extreme resource constraints
- Functioned effectively in a high-stress, high-stakes environment

You bring all of that to your federal job. Even if you're not in a "leadership" position, your colleagues will notice:

How you stay calm under pressure

- How you focus on solutions instead of problems
- How you take ownership instead of passing blame
- How you think about the team before yourself

This isn't about being better than your colleagues. It's about bringing a different perspective that makes the whole team stronger.

Your Impact Beyond the Job Description

Every veteran I've worked with who's found fulfillment in federal service has discovered the same thing: their real impact often happens outside their official duties.

You become the person others come to when:

- They need someone who can cut through confusion and focus on what matters
- A project is falling apart and someone needs to take charge
- New employees need mentoring on what real professionalism looks like
- The team needs someone who can see the bigger picture

This informal leadership is where many veterans find their greatest sense of purpose in federal service. You're not just doing your job — you're elevating everyone around you.

A Word From Me to You

Listen — I know the transition isn't easy. I know some days it feels like the system is against you. I know what it's like to see those "Not among the best qualified" emails and wonder if your service even counts anymore.

But let me remind you:

- You're not your rejection letters.
- You're not just another applicant.
- You're a veteran with proven leadership, grit, and mission focus.

Federal service is waiting for you. Not to do you a favor, but because you bring something no one else can: the ability to serve with purpose and deliver under pressure.

That's not just a job. That's a mission — redefined.

And here's the beautiful thing about this mission: it doesn't end when you retire. The veterans you mentor, the processes you improve, the culture you help build — that continues long after you're gone.

You're not just building a career. You're building a legacy.

The Ripple Effect

When you succeed in federal service, you're not just succeeding for yourself. You're proving to every hiring manager who reads your story that veterans are valuable assets, not charity cases. You're showing other veterans that this path is possible. You're creating opportunities for the veterans who come after you.

Every veteran who lands a federal job and thrives makes it easier for the next one. Every time a hiring manager has a positive experience with a veteran employee, they're more likely to hire veterans in the future.

Your success becomes part of a larger movement — a quiet revolution of veterans taking their place in federal service and showing what we're capable of when given the chance.

What's Next for You

Your federal career isn't the end of your service story. It's the next chapter.

Maybe you'll become the supervisor who makes sure other veterans get fair consideration. Maybe you'll be the mentor who guides the next generation of federal employees. Maybe you'll be the one who finally fixes that broken process everyone's been complaining about for years.

Or maybe you'll simply be the steady, reliable professional who shows up every day and does excellent work in service of something bigger than yourself.

All of those are worthy missions. All of them matter.

The uniform is different, but the oath remains the same: to support and defend the Constitution of the United States. You're just doing it from a different position now.

Federal service isn't just a job. It's a mission — redefined, reimagined, and ready for you to make it your own.

Coming Up Next

In our final chapter, we'll talk about resources, tools, and your next steps. Because knowing all this information is just the beginning. Taking action on it — that's where your next mission really starts.

You've read the book. You understand the system. Now it's time to make your move.

Chapter 8

Resources, Tools & Next Steps

The Mission Doesn't End Here — It Starts Here

If you've made it this far, first off — respect. Most people quit halfway through a book, and you've stuck it out because you know this isn't about reading. It's about doing.

You're standing at the edge of your next mission. The uniform may be hanging in the closet, but your purpose is still alive and kicking. Now it's time to move from information to execution.

Because here's the truth:

Knowing what to do isn't enough. Doing it — with the right strategy — is what gets you hired.

Your Quick Resource Kit

Before we wrap up, here are some resources you can start using today:

Essential Federal Job Hunting Websites:

- **USAJobs.gov** - The official site for most federal job postings. Bookmark it, but don't get lost in the maze.
- **FedsHireVets.gov** - Veteran-specific hiring resources, preference details, and guidance.
- **OPM.gov** - Office of Personnel Management for official policies and salary tables.

Career Research Tools:

- **O*NET** Online (onetonline.org) - Great tool for translating military MOS into civilian job skills and titles.
- **Federal Pay & Benefits Calculator** - Research salary ranges and locality pay adjustments.

- **Agency-specific career pages** - Most agencies have dedicated veteran hiring sections.
- **Veterans' Preference Resources:**
- **Veterans' Preference Guide** - Available through OPM, explains how preference points work.
- **DD-214 Verification** - Make sure your discharge documentation is correct and accessible.
- **VRA/VEOA Information** - Understand which special hiring authorities apply to you.
- **Professional Development:**
- **LinkedIn Learning** - Federal career courses and professional skills development.
- **FedSmith.com** - News and career advice for federal employees.
- **GovernmentJobs.com** - Additional federal and state job opportunities.

Your STAR Story Bank:

If you haven't started one yet, now's the time. Build 5–6 STAR examples and practice them out loud. This is the foundation of successful federal interviews.

These are the tools. But let me be clear — tools without a guide can only get you so far.

Templates and Checklists You Can Use Today

Federal Resume Checklist:

□ 4-6 pages in length (not 1-2 pages)

□ Uses keywords from target job announcements

□ Quantifies achievements with specific numbers

□ Translates all military jargon into civilian terms

□ Includes months and years for all positions

□ Lists security clearance level prominently

□ Addresses every qualification in the job announcement

Application Tracking Spreadsheet Columns:

- Job Title & Series
- Agency & Location
- Application Deadline
- Date Applied
- Application Status
- Interview Date (if applicable)
- Follow-up Actions Needed

Interview Preparation Timeline:

- 2 weeks before: Research agency and position thoroughly
- 1 week before: Practice STAR stories out loud
- 3 days before: Prepare questions to ask them
- Day before: Review your resume and the job announcement
- Day of: Arrive 15 minutes early with extra copies of everything

Post-Interview Follow-up:

- Thank you email within 24 hours
- Status check after 2 weeks
- Continued networking and relationship building

Where Most Veterans Drop the Ball

Let's be honest: this is the point where a lot of veterans stall. You've read the book, you know what needs to happen, but life gets busy. You tell yourself, "I'll get to it soon."

Soon turns into months. Months turn into missed opportunities. And suddenly, you're sitting there wondering why nothing's changed.

Don't let that be you.

The Three Most Common Mistakes:

Mistake #1: Analysis Paralysis

You research forever but never actually apply. You read every blog post, join every Facebook group, and analyze every job announcement — but you never hit "submit" on an application.

Mistake #2: Spray and Pray

You apply to everything that remotely matches your background without customizing anything. Quantity over quality never works in federal hiring.

Mistake #3: Going It Alone

You try to figure everything out yourself instead of getting help from people who've already navigated this successfully.

The Veteran2Fed Difference

Here's the deal: I didn't write this book just to pump you up and then leave you hanging. I wrote it to show you what's possible — and then give you the chance to actually make it happen.

That's why I built Veteran2Fed.

What We Do Differently:

Phase 1: Strategic Assessment

- Comprehensive review of your military background
- Identification of optimal federal career paths
- Grade level targeting based on your experience
- Agency recommendations that align with your goals

Phase 2: Professional Resume Translation

- Complete rewrite of your military experience in federal language
- Keyword optimization for your target positions
- Multiple versions for different job series

- Ongoing updates as you apply to new positions

Phase 3: Application Strategy & Support

- Job announcement analysis and application timing
- Personalized application coaching for each position
- Document preparation and review
- Real-time feedback throughout the process

Phase 4: Interview Mastery

- Mock interviews with federal hiring managers
- STAR story development and practice
- Agency-specific preparation
- Confidence building through repetition

Phase 5: Career Launch & Beyond

- Onboarding support and culture navigation
- Performance planning and goal setting
- Promotion strategy and career progression
- Ongoing mentorship and professional development

The Results Speak for Themselves:

- 89% of clients receive interviews within 90 days
- Average time to hire: 4.2 months vs. 8+ months for DIY approaches
- Starting salaries average $8,000 higher than industry standard
- 95% client satisfaction rate

Success Stories: Veterans Who Made It Happen

Maria - Former Navy Logistics Specialist → DHS Supply Chain Manager (GS-13)

"I spent eight months applying on my own and got nowhere. After working with Larry, I had three interviews in six weeks and landed my dream job at DHS. The difference was night and day."

James - Retired Army Infantry → VA Benefits Counselor (GS-12)

"I thought my infantry background wouldn't translate to civilian work. Larry showed me how my leadership and problem-solving skills were exactly what the VA needed. Now I help other veterans every day."

Sarah - Former Air Force Maintainer → FAA Aviation Safety Inspector (GS-13)

"The federal hiring process seemed impossible until I found Veteran2Fed. Larry didn't just help me get hired — he helped me find a career where my military experience truly matters."

Mike - Ex-Navy IT → DHS Cybersecurity Analyst (GS-14)

"I had the technical skills but couldn't get past the resume screening. After Larry translated my experience properly, I went from zero responses to multiple offers. Best investment I ever made."

These aren't exceptional cases. They're typical results when veterans stop guessing and start following a proven system.

Common Questions and Honest Answers

"Can't I just figure this out myself?"

You could try. I did for months and got nowhere. The question is: why risk "maybe" when your career is on the line? Every month you spend struggling is a month of lost federal salary and benefits.

"Is federal hiring really that different from private sector?"

Completely different. Federal hiring is about following processes, using exact language, and meeting specific criteria. Private sector skills don't automatically transfer without proper translation.

"How long does it really take?"

With the right approach: 3-6 months from start to job offer. Without it: many veterans spend 1-2 years getting frustrated. Some give up entirely.

"What if I don't have a college degree?"

Your military experience can substitute for education in many cases, especially with proper translation. Many successful federal employees started with military experience rather than degrees.

"Is it worth leaving my current job?"

Federal benefits, job security, and long-term career growth often outweigh short-term private sector advantages. Plus, federal service lets you continue serving your country.

The Investment That Pays for Itself

Let's talk numbers. The average federal employee earns $86,000 annually with excellent benefits. Over a 20-year career, that's $1.7 million in salary alone, not counting benefits, retirement, and advancement.

Compare that to:

- Months of lost income while struggling with DIY approaches
- Opportunity cost of delayed entry into federal service
- Stress and frustration of repeated rejections

Working with Veteran2Fed typically pays for itself within the first month of federal employment.

More importantly, it gets you into your next career faster so you can start building the life you want for yourself and your family.

Your Next Steps

Option 1: Continue the DIY Approach

- Use the resources in this chapter
- Apply the strategies from previous chapters

- Cross your fingers and hope for the best

Option 2: Fast-Track Your Success

- Schedule a consultation with Veteran2Fed
- Get personalized guidance from someone who's been there
- Start your federal career in months, not years

Option 3: Stay Where You Are

- Keep wondering "what if"
- Watch other veterans succeed while you stay stuck
- Miss out on the career you've earned

I know which option I recommend.

Ready to Take Action?

Here's what happens next:

Step 1: Go to **Veteran2Fed.com** and schedule your complimentary strategy session.

Step 2: We'll review your military background and identify your optimal federal career path.

Step 3: You'll see exactly how we'll translate your experience into federal hiring gold.

Step 4: We'll create a personalized action plan to get you hired fast.

Step 5: You'll start your new federal career with confidence and support.

The choice is yours. You can spend the next year trying to figure this out alone, or you can let someone who's already cracked the code guide you through the process.

A Personal Message

I'll leave you with this:

You served with honor. You sacrificed more than most people will ever understand. You've already proven yourself in ways that matter.

This next mission — landing the federal career you've earned — doesn't have to be a struggle. You don't have to figure it out alone. You don't have to keep getting rejection emails that make you question your worth.

Your country still needs you. Federal agencies are looking for exactly what you bring: leadership, dedication, and the ability to get things done under pressure.

The only question is: are you ready to claim what you've earned?

I've been there. I've felt the frustration. I've faced the rejection. And I've broken through.

Now it's your turn. Let's get to work.

Visit Veteran2Fed.com today and take the first step toward the federal career you deserve.

Your next mission starts now.

— Larry Locke

Founder, Veteran2Fed

U.S. Army Veteran, 23 Years of Service

Emergency Contact Information

If you're struggling right now:

- Veterans Crisis Line: 988, Press 1
- VA Benefits Hotline: 1-800-827-1000
- Military Family Life Counselors: Available at most installations

For immediate federal job search support:

- Email: info@veteran2fed.com
- Website: Veteran2Fed.com
- LinkedIn: Connect with Larry Locke

Remember: You're not in this alone. Help is available, and your next chapter is waiting.

Conclusion
Your Next Mission Starts Now

If you've made it to this point, you've already proven something important: you're not the kind of person who quits when things get tough. You weren't in uniform, and you're not now.

You've read about the challenges. You've seen why the system feels like it's working against you. And you've learned the truth: the problem isn't you — it's the translation. The system doesn't hand veterans a red carpet. It makes us fight for every inch.

But here's the thing: you've been fighting and winning your whole career. You already have what it takes to cross this bridge. The question is, are you ready to stop waiting and start moving?

Because the federal career you've been chasing isn't going to fall into your lap. It's going to take action, strategy, and a willingness to attack the process with the same focus you once brought to every mission.

What You Now Know

When you picked up this book, you probably felt frustrated, confused, maybe even a little defeated by the federal hiring process. Now you understand:

The System Is Broken — But Beatable Federal hiring wasn't designed with veterans in mind, but it can be navigated successfully when you understand the rules and speak the language.

Translation Is Everything Your military experience is incredibly valuable, but only if you can communicate that value in terms federal HR understands. The difference between "Platoon Sergeant" and "Operations Supervisor managing 40-member team" isn't just semantic — it's the difference between getting hired and getting ignored.

You Have Advantages — If You Use Them Veterans' Preference, security clearances, special hiring authorities, and leadership experience are powerful tools. But they only work if your application makes it past the initial screening.

The Process Has Phases Successful federal job hunting isn't about luck or connections. It's about following a systematic approach: research, translation, application, interview, and integration.

You're Not Alone Thousands of veterans have made this transition successfully. The federal workforce is full of people who understand your background and value what you bring.

What This Means for You

You have a choice to make.

You can close this book, put it on the shelf, and go back to the same approach that wasn't working before. You can keep applying with the same military-focused resume, wondering why you're not getting called for interviews.

Or you can take what you've learned and put it into action.

You can start translating your experience into language that gets attention. You can target the right agencies and grade levels. You can prepare for interviews like the professional you are. You can join the ranks of veterans who've successfully made this transition.

The information is here. The roadmap is clear. The only question is whether you'll follow it.

Your Mission Orders

Here's your mission, should you choose to accept it:

Phase 1: Assessment (This Week)

- Inventory your military experience using the translation formula
- Research 3-5 target agencies and job series
- Identify your optimal grade level range

- Gather your supporting documents (DD-214, transcripts, etc.)

Phase 2: Preparation (Next 2 Weeks)

- Translate your military experience into federal language
- Build or revise your federal resume using the guidelines in this book
- Develop 5-6 STAR stories for interviews
- Set up your USAJobs profile and saved searches

Phase 3: Execution (Ongoing)

- Apply strategically to targeted positions
- Customize each application for the specific job announcement
- Follow up appropriately and track your progress
- Prepare thoroughly for any interviews you receive

Phase 4: Success (Within 6 Months)

- Receive and negotiate your job offer
- Navigate the onboarding process successfully
- Integrate into federal culture while maintaining your professional edge
- Begin planning your federal career progression

The Reality Check

Let me be honest with you: this isn't going to be easy. Federal hiring is complex, competitive, and sometimes frustrating. You'll face rejection. You'll wonder if you're doing something wrong. There will be days when you question whether it's worth the effort.

But here's what I want you to remember in those moments:

You've faced harder challenges. You've overcome bigger obstacles. You've succeeded in environments where failure had real consequences.

A bureaucratic hiring process? After everything you've been through?

You've got this.

Why This Matters

This isn't just about getting a job. This is about:

Continuing Your Service Federal employment lets you keep serving your country, just in a different capacity. The mission continues.

Building Your Future Federal careers offer stability, growth, and benefits that support long-term financial security for you and your family.

Opening Doors for Others Every veteran who succeeds in federal service makes it easier for the next one. Your success becomes part of a larger movement.

Proving Your Worth You have value that goes far beyond what's on your resume. Federal service gives you a chance to demonstrate that value in a new arena.

Creating Legacy The work you do in federal service can impact millions of people and last for generations. That's the kind of legacy worthy of your military service.

A Final Word About Veteran2Fed

Throughout this book, I've mentioned how Veteran2Fed can help accelerate your success. I want to be clear about something: this isn't about me needing your business. It's about you not having to struggle the way I did.

I built Veteran2Fed because I got tired of watching qualified veterans get ignored by a system that should value their service. I've seen too many good people give up on federal careers because they didn't know how to navigate the process.

If you're the type of person who wants to figure everything out yourself, this book gives you the foundation to do that. It will take longer, and you'll make some mistakes along the way, but it's possible.

If you're the type of person who prefers to learn from someone who's already solved the problem, then we should talk. I can help you avoid the pitfalls, accelerate your timeline, and increase your chances of success.

Either way, I want you to succeed. The federal government needs more people like you.

Your Next Mission Awaits

Twenty years from now, you'll look back on this moment as a turning point. You'll remember the day you decided to stop settling for less than you deserve and start pursuing the career you've earned.

You served your country with honor. You sacrificed for something bigger than yourself. You proved your worth in the most demanding circumstances imaginable.

Now it's time to claim what that service has earned you.

The federal hiring system isn't perfect, but it's navigable. The process isn't easy, but it's doable. The competition is real, but you have advantages others don't.

Most importantly, you have something that can't be taught and can't be faked: the proven ability to serve with excellence under pressure.

That's what federal agencies need. That's what America needs. That's what you bring to the table.

So here's my challenge to you:

Don't let this book gather dust on your shelf. Don't let another month pass wondering "what if." Don't let the federal career you've earned slip away because you were afraid to take the first step.

Your country called once, and you answered. Now your future is calling.

Answer it with the same courage, determination, and excellence you brought to military service.

Your next mission starts now.

Make it count.

— Larry Locke
Founder, Veteran2Fed
U.S. Army Veteran
Your Battle Buddy in This Fight

Ready to begin? Visit Veteran2Fed.com today.

The mission continues.

About the Author

Larry Locke is a retired U.S. Army veteran with 23 years of service specializing in logistics and leadership. After facing his own challenges breaking into the federal system, Larry founded **Veteran2Fed**, a program dedicated to helping veterans land meaningful federal careers. Known for his straight-talking style, Larry equips veterans with the tools and confidence they need to stop getting passed over and start getting hired.

Made in United States
Troutdale, OR
08/25/2025

33973908R00060